A Guide to the Normandy of Saint Thérèse

CHRISTINE FROST

The Theresian Trust
and St Thérèse Missionary League
in association with Anthony Clarke
1994

Co-Published by
The Theresian Trust
617 Church Road
Yardley
Birmingham B33 8HA
England

&

St. Thérèse Missionary League
P.O. Box 1406
Dublin 8
Ireland

In association with
Anthony Clarke
Wheathampstead
Hertfordshire
England

First published 1994

ISBN 0 85650 123 9

Quotations from *Story of a Soul* translated by John Clarke, O.C.D.
© 1975, 1976 by Washington Province Discalced Carmelites
ICS Publications 2131 Lincoln Road, N.E. Washington D.C. U.S.A.

Media conversion and outputting by
Diskon Technical Services Ltd.,
48 Reuben Avenue, Dublin 8.
Designed and printed in the
Republic of Ireland by
Elo Press Ltd.,
49 Reuben Avenue, Rialto, Dublin 8.
Cover design by Kevin O'Neill
Photography by Christine Frost

CONTENTS

FOREWORD

Alençon, where Saint Thérèse was born, and Lisieux, where she spent most of her life, are the most important places for the pilgrim. These towns are both accessible by train from all the French ports, though it may be necessary to change trains, and details of your individual journey should be checked with French Railways or with your travel agent. When travelling from Lisieux to Alençon by train, it is usually necessary to change at Mezidon. It is possible to visit Alençon, Sées, Trouville and Deauville, Bayeux and Caen on day returns from Lisieux.

Train services are usually good in France and run on time, but it is always advisable to check details of public transport locally. This applies especially to local buses.

All the places mentioned in this guide are easily reached by car from Lisieux or Alençon and road directions are given for each journey. All the towns and most of the smaller places are well marked on the Michelin map 231 'France Normandie'.

If the weather is fine and you have plenty of time and enjoy walking you will be able to visit the places near Lisieux on foot. Unfortunately at the time of writing there is only a weekly bus from Lisieux to St.-Ouen le Pin and it is a long walk from Lisieux.

INTRODUCTION

Another book on St. Thérèse? Fewer saints in the Church have had so much written about them than "The Greatest Saint of Modern Times" (Pope St. Pius X. Pope Pius XI). Yet, I feel this is the book that has been missing! This guide book is an invaluable contribution to Theresian literature.

Arguably, the greatest theologian of the twentieth-century, Cardinal Hans Urs Von Balthasar, in his *Thérèse of Lisieux – The Story of a Mission* reminds us that "because of the depth of revealed truth, portraits of the saints must in future be remodelled, so that the saints can again live amongst us, and in us, as the best protectors and inspirers of the community of the saints which is the Church".

Christine Frost ably assisted by her husband, Maurice, and Marie O'Grady co-trustees with me of the international Theresian Trust, has spent all of fourteen years meticulously researching every detail.

Obviously, as the book will show, she deals only in facts and gives us a wonderful picture of the background to St. Thérèse. Many authors have dealt with specific areas of the saint's homeland. This excellent book provides a complete guide for all those visiting St. Thérèse's Normandy, whether for the first time or on a return visit. Motor traffic to France from the European mainland, England and Ireland, has greatly increased in recent years. The advent of the new England to France 'chunnel' will greatly add to the numbers, who by design or chance follow the roadsigns to Lisieux. This book will not only direct them to all the places associated with the saint, but it will also, for those who do not know St. Thérèse, give a clear introduction to her life and thought. Devotees of St. Thérèse will be able to follow in her steps and will recognise some familiar passages from her writings. Reading about an event where it actually took place will add an extra dimension to the experience. Those wanting more detailed information about St. Thérèse's family and the less well-known places connected with her will find it here.

At the time of printing – March 1994 – we feel this book will make a vital contribution to the success of the celebrations for the Centenary of the death of St. Thérèse, September 1997. The ever increasing movement to have the Lisieux Carmelite – Universal Patron of all Missions and Missionaries – declared a Doctor of the Church will find much support from this book.

Happily also as we go to press, we rejoice in the wonderful news that the formal decree by His Holiness Pope John Paul II affirming the heroic virtues of the parents of St. Thérèse, Louis and Zélie, has just been officially announced, 26th March, 1994, by the Vatican. This wonderful news comes during the International Year of the Family and during the Centenary Year (July 29th) of Louis Martin's death.

Christine and Maurice Frost should be warmly congratulated on the excellence of this vital contribution towards an even greater devotion to St. Thérèse. They, in turn, know that their work could not have seen the light of day without the generous help of St. Thérèse Missionary league, P.O. Box 1406, Dublin 8, Ireland. Congratulations also to Elo Press, South Circular Road, Dublin on the excellence of their printing and layout. may this following in the geographical footsteps of St. Thérèse place us firmly on her Little Way, which unerringly leads to heaven.

J. Linus Ryan, O. Carm.,
Prior.
Carmelites,
White Abbey,
Kildare Town,
Ireland.

The Family of St. Thérèse

Louis Joseph Aloys Stanislaus Martin = **Zélie Marie Guérin**
B. August 22nd 1823 Bordeaux   B. December 23rd 1831 St.
    Denis-sur-Sarthon
    M. July 13th 1858   Alençon
D. July 29th 1894 La Musse, Evreux   D. August 28th 1877 Alençon

Marie Louise
B. February 22nd 1860 Alençon
Entered Carmel of Lisieux October 15th 1886
Sr. Marie of the Sacred Heart D. January 19th 1940

Marie Pauline
B. September 7th 1861 Alençon
Entered Carmel of Lisieux October 2nd 1882
Sr. Agnes of Jesus D. July 28th 1951

Marie Léonie
B. June 3rd 1863 Alençon
Entered Visitation of Caen January 29th 1899
Sr. Françoise Thérèse D. June 16th 1941

Marie Hélène
B. October 13th 1864 Alençon
D. February 22nd 1870

Marie Joseph Louis
B. September 20th 1866 Alençon
D. February 14th 1867

Marie Joseph Jean Baptiste
B. December 19th 1867 Alençon
D. August 24th 1868

Marie Céline
B. April 28th 1869 Alençon
Entered Carmel of Lisieux September 14th 1894
Sr. Geneviève of St. Teresa D. February 25th 1959

Marie Melanie Thérèse
B. August 17th 1870 Alençon
D. October 8th 1870

Marie Françoise Thérèse
B. January 2nd 1873 Alençon
Entered carmel of Lisieux April 9th 1888
Sr. Thérèse of the Child Jesus and of the Holy Face
D. September 30th 1897
St. Thérèse of Lisieux - Canonised May 17th 1925

The Family of Zélie Guérin
Mother of St. Thérèse

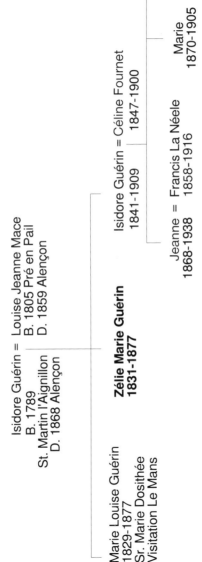

Isidore Guérin = Louise Jeanne Mace
B. 1789   B. 1805 Pré en Pail
St. Martin l'Aignillon   D. 1859 Alençon
D. 1868 Alençon

Zélie Marie Guérin
1831-1877

Isidore Guérin = Céline Fournet
1841-1909   1847-1900

Marie Louise Guérin
1829-1877
Sr. Marie Dosithée
Visitation Le Mans

Jeanne = Francis La Néele
1868-1938   1858-1916

Marie
1870-1905

Paul
1871

Isidore and Céline Guérin were married in 1866. Their only son, Paul, was still born. Their daughter Marie became Sr. Marie of the Eucharist in the Carmel of Lisiux.

The Family of Louis Martin

Father of St. Thérèse

Anne Fannie Boureau = Pierre François Martin
B. 1800 Blois   B. 1777 Athis
D. 1883   M. 1818   D. 1865 Alençon
                         (Capitaine)

Pierre Martin
B. 1819 Nantes
Died at Sea.

Marie Anne Martin
1820-1846
M. François Burin

Louis Joseph Aloys
Stanislaus Martin
1823-1894

Anne Fannie Martin = Adolphe Leriche
B. 1826 Avignon   1818-1843
D. 1853

Adolphe Leriche
1844-1894
(To whom Louis sold his watchmaker
and jewellers shop.)

Sophie
(Died)
(Aged 9)

LISIEUX

CARMEL

Thérèse entered Carmel on April 9th. 1888 at the age of fifteen, she remained there until she died at the age of twenty-four on September 30th. 1897.

The public chapel of Carmel is adjoining the monastery at 37, rue du Carmel. The Carmel of Lisieux was founded in 1838. Thérèse had difficulty in obtaining permission to enter Carmel at the age of fifteen, but she was convinced of her vocation and supported by her father. Her sisters, Pauline and Marie had entered before her and on the death of their father, in 1894, another sister, Céline, joined them. Thérèse's cousin Marie Guérin also entered the Carmel of Lisieux. In all there were twenty-six nuns at Carmel when Thérèse entered; this included five lay sisters and two externs. The community today is smaller; there are no longer lay sisters, but externs continue to play an important part.

It is possible to assist at the Community Mass at 9 a.m. each day, and it is usually possible to join the sisters for part of the Divine Office at 7.15 a.m., 1.45 p.m. and 5 p.m. There is also Mass in the Carmelite Chapel at 8 a.m. and 11.30 a.m. each day.

When Thérèse entered Carmel the Prioress showed her the different places in the community, and Thérèse later wrote:

Everything, thrilled me; I felt as though I was transported into a desert; our little cell, above all, filled me with joy... Ah! I was fully recompensed for all my trials. With what deep joy I repeated those words: 'I am here forever and ever!'

Lisieux

1 Carmel
2 Les Buissonets
3 The Cathedral
4 The Benedictine Convent
5 St. Jacques
6 Public Gardens
7 The Guérin Pharmacy
8 The Guérin House
9 The Martin House
10 The Basilica
11 The Belvedere
12 The Cemetery

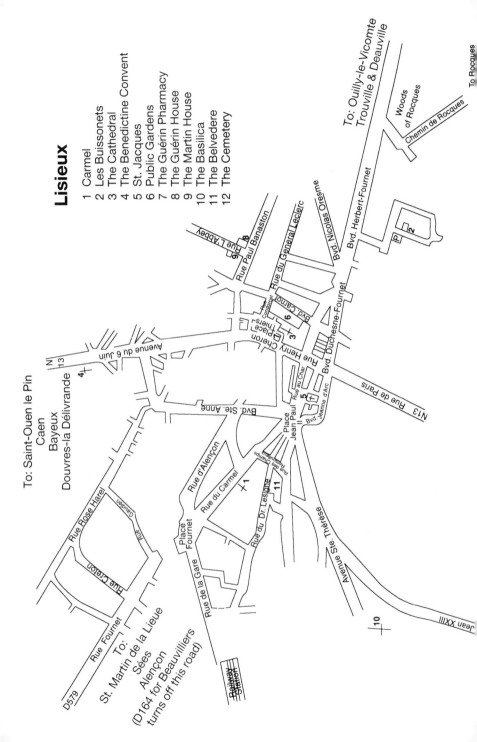

The Carmelite Chapel and the monastery have been extended since Thérèse's day. She recalls her first visit with her father when she was six years old:

'Each afternoon I took a walk with Papa. We made our visit to the Blessed Sacrament together, going to a different church each day, and it was in this way we entered the Carmelite Chapel for the first time. Papa showed me the choir grille and told me that there were nuns behind it. I was far from thinking at the time that nine years later I would be in their midst!

As you enter the Carmelite Chapel, St. Thérèse's Shrine is to your right, about halfway down. Her recumbent statue contains some relics, but most of them are kept in a reliquary in the vault below. The golden rose in Thérèse's hand was given by Pope Pius XI. This is the most important place of prayer for the pilgrim to Lisieux. Many pilgrims place flowers through the grating and these are used to decorate the Shrine area. Kneeling at the Shrine it is easy to be aware of Thérèse's desire to spend her heaven doing good on earth, helping souls to love God as she loved Him.

The coat of arms at the top of the casket is a copy of one which Thérèse drew for herself. The initials above on the left are *JHS* the first three letters of the name of Jesus in Greek, and on the right *MFT* the initial letters of Thérèse's three baptismal names Marie Françoise Thérèse. The left side shows the Child Jesus and the Holy Face, her titles in religion. The harp represents Thérèse, who wishes to sing unceasingly of her love for Jesus. On the right is the little flower, Thérèse, receiving the beneficent rays of the morning star, Our Lady. The rich soil of Thérèse's childhood and the mountain of Carmel are also represented. The final section shows the dart of love which wins the palm of martyrdom and above is the luminous triangle of the Blessed Trinity. Thérèse's motto taken from St. John of the Cross reads: *Love is repaid by love alone.*

Map of Mainline Railways
and Towns in Northern France

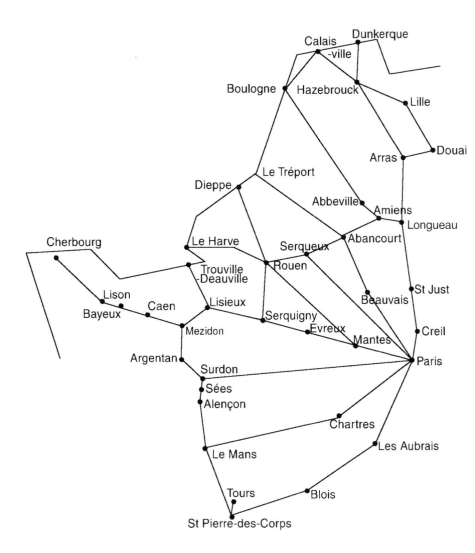

High above the Shrine is the statue of Our Lady of the Smile, a copy of Bouchardon's Madonna. This is the actual statue which smiled on Thérèse on May 13th. 1883.

Each year on the last weekend of September, the Feast of St. Thérèse is celebrated in Lisieux. Her relics are taken from the vault and placed in the Brazilian Reliquary. On Saturday evening after opening prayers and hymns in Carmel, the reliquary is taken in a candlelit procession through the streets of Lisieux to the Basilica. High Mass is celebrated on Sunday morning and in the afternoon the procession returns to Carmel by way of the Cathedral.

On the approach to the Shrine there is a small altar on each side. These were both given by Canon T. N. Taylor, a Scotsman, and one of the early translators of *Story of a Soul*; he was also one of the witnesses in the tribunal for Thérèse's beatification. The altar on the left is dedicated to the Child Jesus; the statue is a copy of one in the cloister which Thérèse used to decorate with candles and flowers. The altar to the right is dedicated to the Holy Face. Above each altar there is a window depicting one of the early miracles. On the left Thérèse is seen appearing on one of the battlefields of the First World War, where a soldier in the trenches is healed. On the right she is appearing to a missionary priest in the Congo; his healing took place in 1919. Two of the windows in the main Chapel depict events from Thérèse's life, one shows her kneeling at the feet of Pope Leo XIII and another shows her kneeling to receive her father's blessing on the day of her Clothing.

The nuns' choir is to the right of the main altar. Thérèse sat in a stall to the left and it is marked with a cross. On the sanctuary in front of the nuns' choir are the tombs of two of the founders of Carmel, Father Pierre-Nicolas Sauvage (1794-1853) and Mother Geneviève of St. Teresa (1805-1891). Thérèse wrote of the death of Mother Geneviève:

> *The memory which Mother Geneviève left in my heart is a sacred memory. The day of her departure for Heaven, I was particularly touched; it was the*

first time I had assisted at a death and really the spectacle was ravishing. I was placed at the foot of the dying saint's bed, and witnessed her slightest movements. During the two hours I spent there, it seemed to me that my soul should have been filled with fervour; however, a sort of insensibility took control of me. But at the moment itself of our saintly Mother Geneviève's birth into Heaven, my interior disposition changed and in the twinkling of an eye I experienced an inexpressible joy and fervour; it was as though Mother Geneviève had imparted to me a little of the happiness she was enjoying, for I was convinced she went straight to Heaven.

The side aisle has been added since St. Thérèse's time but the statues of St. Teresa of Avila and St. John of the Cross now found there stood on either side of the main altar at the time of St. Thérèse.

Outside the Chapel, to the left of the main door as you leave, you will see a plaque on the wall indicating that St. Thérèse's three Carmelite sisters are laid to rest in the vaults of Carmel, beneath the Shrine Chapel. Marie (Sister Marie of the Sacred Heart) died in 1940, Pauline (Mother Agnes of Jesus) in 1951 and Céline (Sister Geneviève of the Holy Face) in 1959.

On the opposite side of the courtyard there is a small shop where photographs of St. Thérèse, prayer cards, postcards, etc. are on sale.

The entrance to the **Hall of Relics** is beside the shop. Here objects relevant to Thérèse's life in Carmel are displayed in a number of showcases around the walls. A ten minute pre-recorded commentary in eight languages, including English, is available for 1 Franc from a machine on the left as you enter, it is necessary to hear the commentary as this works in conjunction with the lights in the various showcases.

Outside the Chapel railings, in the garden to the right,

St. Thérèse's shrine in Carmel.

The Hall of Relics. In the last showcase, the palm which was buried with St. Thérèse and found to be still fresh and green at her exhumation, is still wonderfully preserved.

The Carmel of Lisieux.

Les Buissonnets.
Home of St. Thérèse
from 1877-1888.

Les Buissonnets.
A sculptured group in the
garden marks the place
where Thérèse asked her
father for his permission to
enter Carmel.

18

there is a traditional white statue of St. Thérèse, made by the Trappist sculptor Father Marie-Bernard.

Opposite the Chapel, you will find the Librairie du Carmel – Office Central. This is the main shop selling books and photographs of St. Thérèse.

LES BUISSONNETS

Thérèse's home from the age of 4½ until she entered Carmel at the age of 15 (1877-1888)

To reach Les Buissonnets take the D579, the Deauville/Trouville road, called at first Boulevard Jeanne d'Arc and leading into Boulevard Duchesne-Fournet and Herbet-Fournet, a narrow turning off to the right leads to the

Les Buissonnets: Reconstruction of Thérèse's little crib in a niche in the wash-house wall.

house. It is well sign-posted and a statue of St. Thérèse can be seen from the main road. Immediately past the statue there is a car park to the right. Turn right between the car park and the souvenir shop up a narrow lane, which remains as it was in Thérèse's time. Les Buissonnets is the first house on the left, it is surrounded by high walls and is entered through a tall gate which leads into the front garden with lawn, trees and flower beds. Straight ahead is the red brick house, three floors at the front and two at the back.

Thérèse wrote:

> *At Les Buissonnets my life was truly happy... the affection with which I was surrounded helped me to grow.*

Before entering the house observe the attic windows. In Thérèse's time the central room was known as the Belvedere. It was there that Louis Martin, Thérèse's father, had his study. Before Thérèse started school her sisters, Marie and Pauline, taught her at home and, after her lessons for the day were over, she loved to climb the stairs to report her progress to her father. Later Thérèse and Céline, the sister nearest to her in age, held spiritual conversations there. Thérèse wrote of them:

> *How sweet were the conversations we held each evening in the Belvedere! With enraptured gaze we beheld the white moon rising quietly behind the tall trees, the silvery rays it was casting upon sleeping nature, the bright stars twinkling in the deep skies, the light breath of the evening breeze making the snowy clouds float easily along; all this raised our souls to Heaven, that beautiful Heaven whose 'obverse side' alone we were able to contemplate.*

In another of these attics Pauline had her painting room and after she had entered Carmel Thérèse made this her own.

Now enter the house, it is under the care of the Oblates of St. Thérèse and if you tell them you are English speaking they will put on a cassette to guide you through the various rooms.

The first room you enter was the kitchen, which served also as the living room. You will see the fireplace where Thérèse left her shoes each Christmas Eve, so that they would be filled with presents for her to open on returning from Midnight Mass. One such occasion marked a turning point in her life. Ever since the death of her mother, Thérèse had cried very easily and she had begged God to deliver her from this failing. She wrote of that night:

> It was December 25th, 1886, that I received the grace of leaving my childhood, in a word, the grace of my complete conversion. We had come back from Midnight Mass where I had the happiness of receiving the strong and powerful God. Upon arriving at Les Buissonnets, I used to love to take my shoes from the chimney-corner and examine the presents in them... However, Jesus desired to show me that I was to give up the defects of my childhood... He permitted Papa, tired out after the Midnight Mass, to experience annoyance when seeing my shoes in the fireplace, and that he speak those words which pierced my heart: 'Well, fortunately, this will be the last year!

Thérèse, who would normally have burst into tears at such a remark, found that she had the strength to open her presents joyfully and soon her father was laughing too. She later wrote:

> On that night of light began the third period of my life, the most beautiful and filled with graces from Heaven. The work I had been unable to do in ten years was done by Jesus in one instant.

On a wall in this room there is a painting of Les Buissonnets by Céline.

Through a window to the right of the fireplace it is possible to look into the dining room where the main meals were taken, though breakfast was eaten in the kitchen. It was here that Thérèse had her farewell meal the night before she entered Carmel. The clock on the mantelpiece was made by Louis Martin.

Going up the stairs you enter the bedroom which was used by Marie and Pauline. It is the room in which Marie cared for Thérèse when she was suffering from a mysterious illness, shortly after Pauline entered Carmel. It was in this room that Thérèse was suddenly and miraculously cured on May 13th. 1883 when Our Lady smiled on her. A copy of the statue stands on a chest of drawers beside the bed.

Thérèse wrote:

> *Marie knelt down near my bed with Léonie and Céline. Turning to the Blessed Virgin and praying with the fervour of a mother begging for the life of her child, Marie obtained what she wanted. Finding no help on earth, poor little Thérèse had also turned towards the Mother of Heaven, and prayed with all her heart that she take pity on her. All of a sudden the Blessed Virgin appeared beautiful to me, so beautiful that never had I seen anything so attractive; her face was suffused with an ineffable benevolence and tenderness, but what penetrated to the very depths of my soul was the ravishing smile of the Blessed Virgin.*

After Marie entered Carmel in October 1886 Thérèse and Céline slept in this room.

Through a window next to the room of Our Lady of the Smile it is possible to look into Louis Martin's bedroom. The painting reflected in the mirror shows Our Lady consoling St. Mary Magdalene; it was painted by Céline, and inspired her father to offer her art lessons in Paris. However, Céline declined as she had already decided to enter Carmel. The lamps on the mantelpiece were used at the evening meal on the day Thérèse made her First Holy Communion, May 8th. 1884.

The last room you enter was the bedroom shared by Thérèse and Céline until Marie entered Carmel. It was here that Thérèse liked to go behind her bed-curtain to pray. She wrote:

One day, one of my teachers at the Abbey asked me what I did on my free afternoons when I was alone. I told her I went behind my bed in an empty space which was there, and that it was easy to close myself in with my bed-curtain and that I thought. 'But what do you think about?' she asked. I told her I thought about God, about life and about eternity.

Around this room there are paintings showing scenes from Thérèse's childhood.

Behind a large glass window objects from Thérèse's childhood are displayed, in what was Léonie's bedroom. Thérèse's First Communion dress, the dress she wore for Sundays and Feast days when she was 7-8 years old, some of her school books and many of the toys she used can be seen. These include the skipping rope which she is holding on a photograph taken with Céline in 1881, the cups in which she used to make mixtures from seeds and bark and the miniature altar with crucifix, candles, monstrance, censer and bell. On the right is the crucifix before which she prayed for the conversion of Henri Pranzini, a convicted murderer who refused to repent, but at the last moment kissed the crucifix.

Also on display on the left is the little boat which Céline gave to Thérèse on Christmas night 1887. Thérèse wrote:

When I returned from Midnight Mass I found in my room, a little boat carrying the little Jesus asleep with a little ball at his side, and Céline had written these words on the white sail: 'I sleep but my heart watches', and on the boat itself this one word, 'Abandonment!'

Passing through a door you are in the back garden, where on May 29th 1887 Thérèse asked her father for his permission to enter Carmel. A sculptured group marks the place where she made her request. It was on this occasion that he gave her the little white flower which was to become the symbol of her life. She kept it in her copy of *The Imitation of Christ* and when, years later, Pauline asked her to write her childhood memories she entitled them 'The Springtime Story of a Little White Flower'. It is for this reason that Thérèse is often referred to as The Little Flower.

At the end of the garden in a recess in the wash house wall, a little crib has been reconstructed using the same figures which Thérèse used. Her own patch of garden was in front of this wall. She wrote:

> *I loved cultivating my little flowers in the garden Papa gave me. I amused myself, too, by setting up little altars in a niche in the middle of the wall.*

To the right of the wash house is an aviary which reminds us that Thérèse liked to keep pet birds.Following the paths to the left of the house it is easy to imagine the girls playing in the garden. The ivy reminds us of Céline's last visit to Les Buissonnets on December 23rd. 1889, – the lease expired on Christmas Day – when she picked some ivy leaves, one of which she sent to Thérèse in Carmel, *The souvenir of so many souvenirs.*

Following the path round you can look down into a recess in the wall on the left side of the house, where you will see a sculpture depicting St Thérèse kneeling by the Cross, with the Child Jesus and the Veil of the Holy Face.

Thérèse wrote:

> *At Les Buissonnets my life passed by tranquilly and happily.*

She left this happy home of her childhood on April 9th. 1888 when she entered Carmel. She wrote of that day:

> *On the morning of that great day, casting a last look upon Les Buissonnets, that beautiful cradle of my childhood which I was never to see again, I left on my dear King's arm to climb Mount Carmel.*

The Cathedral of St. Pierre
The High Altar donated by Louis Martin in 1888.

THE CATHEDRAL OF SAINT PIERRE

The Martin family assisted at Mass here every Sunday and frequently on week days. They also went to Sunday Vespers. Thérèse made her first confession here. Isidore Guérin was a churchwarden of St. Pierre.

The Cathedral is situated in the market square, Place Thiers. It is built in the Gothic Norman style.

Thérèse was referring to the Cathedral when she wrote:

All along the way to church and even in the church Papa's little Queen (Thérèse) held his hand. Her place was by his side, and when we had to go down into the body of the church to listen to the sermon, two chairs had to be found side by side... Uncle, sitting in the wardens' pews, was always happy to see us come.

As you enter the Cathedral go over to the north (left) aisle and walk towards the main altar. In the first side chapel, the Chapel of the Annunciation near the back of the Cathedral, you will see the confessional where Thérèse went frequently to confession and where she made her first confession at the age of seven. Thérèse wrote of this occasion:

Well instructed in all I had to say and do, I entered the confessional and knelt down. On opening the grating Father Ducellier saw no one. I was so little my head was below the arm rest. He told me to stand up... I received his blessing with great devotion for you (Pauline) had told me that at the moment he gave me the absolution the tears of Jesus were going to purify my soul.

The High Altar was donated by Louis Martin in 1888, as stated on a plaque behind it. Thérèse recalls this gift: *Papa had just made a donation to God of an altar, and it was he who was chosen as a victim to be offered with the Lamb without spot.* Thérèse was referring here to the onset of her father's illness. Above the High Altar there are three modern stained glass windows – the one on the right depicts St. Thérèse.

In the Lady Chapel, where the Blessed Sacrament is reserved, there is a plaque on the left wall at the back, recalling Thérèse's presence here at weekday Masses. Thérèse loved to pray in this chapel and it was here particularly, in the summer of 1887, that she prayed fervently for the conversion of Henri Pranzini. Thérèse was deeply impressed by the bas-relief on the wall to the left of the altar, depicting Our Lord crucified between the two thieves. This inspired her with confidence that if Pranzini repented, even at the last minute, he would be received into paradise like the good thief. The chapel was built by Pierre Cauchon, Bishop of Lisieux, in reparation for his part in St. Joan of Arc's trial, and he is interred here.

Les Buissonnets. The room where Thérèse was cured when Our Lady smiled on her.

Les Buissonnets. The fireplace where Thérèse left her shoes each Christmas Eve.

The Cathedral of St. Pierre and to the right the (rebuilt) Guérin Pharmacy.

The Church of St. Jacques (now an exhibition hall).

*The Cathedral of St. Pierre.
'The Guardian Angel' by
Céline's art teacher,
Edouard Krug.*

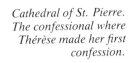

*Cathedral of St. Pierre.
The confessional where
Thérèse made her first
confession.*

*The Cemetery. The statue of St. Thérèse which marks
the place of her second grave.*

The Cathedral of St. Pierre.

Passing round on the south side you come immediately to the chapel where Thérèse used to sit with her father for Sunday Mass up to the time of the sermon. Three plaques and a modern statue of St. Thérèse by J. Lambert Rucki are found in this chapel. Here on December 25th. 1886 at Midnight Mass, Thérèse received a special grace, which she discovered on returning home to Les Buissonnets. (See page 21). On that night her missionary vocation began. She wrote:

> *He (Jesus) made me a fisher of souls. I experienced a great desire to work for the conversion of sinners, a desire I hadn't felt so intensely before. I felt charity enter my soul, and the need to forget myself and please others; since then I've been happy!*

In this chapel the following July (1887) Thérèse's apostolic vocation was confirmed, when, as she closed her missal, a picture of the crucifixion slipped from the pages.
She wrote:

> *One Sunday, looking at a picture of Our Lord on the Cross, I was struck by the blood flowing from one of the divine hands. I felt a great pang of sorrow when thinking that this blood was falling to the ground without anyone's hastening to gather it up. I was resolved to remain in spirit at the foot of the Cross and to receive the divine dew. I understood I was then to pour it out upon souls. The cry of Jesus on the Cross sounded continually in my heart: 'I thirst!' These words ignited within me an unknown and very living fire. I wanted to give my Beloved to drink and I felt myself consumed with a thirst for souls.*

Continuing on down the south side you pass another door to the Cathedral, this was the one most used by the Martin family. In the first of the side chapels past the wide entrance area, you will find a nineteenth century statue of Our Lady of Mount Carmel which was recovered from the ruins of the Church of St. Jacques in 1944. It was before this statue that Pauline received the revelation of her Carmelite vocation. (See page 35).

In the next side chapel there is a painting 'The Guardian Angel' by Edouard Krug (1875). This Norman painter gave lessons to Céline and wanted her to study art in Paris, but she refused because she knew her vocation was to Carmel. After she entered, he often visited her in the parlour and encouraged her to continue with her art.

Finally, just before the main door, you come to the baptistry, where Thérèse's cousins, Jeanne and Marie Guérin, were baptised. Their parents, Isidore Guérin and Céline Fournet had been married in the Cathedral on September 11th. 1866.

THE BENEDICTINE CONVENT
Abbaye Notre Dame du Pré,
36, avenue du 6 juin.

**Thérèse went to school here from October 1881
when she was eight and a half years old until
March 1886 when she was thirteen.**

The original building was completely destroyed in 1944, when
twenty of the community of sixty were killed as a result of the
air raids on the night of 7th-8th June.

A Benedictine Convent had stood on this site since the
time of William the Conqueror, who signed the charter for its
foundation in 1046. After its destruction in 1944 the convent
was rebuilt. The school had already closed in 1904. In 1954
the new convent provided a hostel, where many pilgrims have
been accommodated.

It is interesting that of all the places closely connected with
St. Thérèse, this is the only one which did not survive the
1944 raids.

Thérèse was never happy at school; she wrote:

> *I was eight and a half when Léonie left boarding
> school and I replaced her at the Abbey. I have often
> heard it said that the time spent at school is the best
> and happiest of one's life. It wasn't this way for me.
> The five years I spent in school were the saddest in
> my life.*

In spite of her unhappiness at school, it was here that she
experienced the *beautiful day of days*, when she received her
First Holy Communion. At the back of the modern public
chapel, an altar dedicated to St. Thérèse stands on the place
where she made her First Holy Communion on May 8th.
1884, and above it a painting depicts the event, showing the

young Thérèse with Our Lady and the Child Jesus. Thérèse recalling her First Communion Day wrote:

> *Ah! how sweet was that first kiss of Jesus! It was a kiss of love; I felt that I was loved, and I said: 'I love You, and I give myself to You forever!' There were no demands made, no struggles, no sacrifices; for a long time now Jesus and poor little Thérèse looked at and understood each other. That day, it was no longer simply a look, it was a fusion; they were no longer two, Thérèse had vanished as a drop of water is lost in the immensity of the ocean. Jesus alone remained.*

That same year on June 14th. Thérèse received the Sacrament of Confirmation. She appreciated the retreat beforehand spent at the school. She wrote:

> *A short time after my First Communion, I entered upon another retreat for my Confirmation, I was prepared with great care to receive the visit of the Holy Spirit, and I did not understand why greater attention was not paid to the reception of this sacrament of Love. Ordinarily, there was only one day of retreat made for Confirmation, but the Bishop was unable to come on the appointed day and so I had the consolation of having two days of solitude.*

Thérèse's last contact with the school was in the spring of 1887 when she returned for two afternoons each week in order to be received into the Association of the Children of Mary; she was admitted on May 31st. 1887.

A number of souvenirs of Thérèse's school days are on display in a glass case in the entrance hall of the convent. Some of these were salvaged from the ruins of the old Abbey. It is usually necessary to ring the bell at the main door of the convent. The souvenirs are directly opposite this door. A sister will put on the light in the case for you and if you tell her you are English speaking she will give you the English script describing the contents, which include some First Communion cards, photographs and part of Thérèse's school uniform.

N.B. The above was correct in early 1994 but plans are being made for the Benedictine nuns to move to Valmont and it is not yet known what will happen to the souvenirs of St. Thérèse. Pilgrims are advised to check at the pilgrimage office at 31, rue du Carmel.

THE CHURCH OF SAINT JACQUES
rue au Char

Parish Church of the Martin Family.

This church (St. James) dates from 1540 and was reconstructed in its original style after it was damaged in the 1944 raids. It is no longer used as a church but provides the modern town of Lisieux with an exhibition hall. It is now in the hands of the municipal authorities.

The Martin family never attended this church on Sundays because there were no vacant pews at the time of their arrival in Lisieux. However, they often assisted at weekday Masses here and it was here that Pauline discovered her Carmelite vocation, on February 16th, 1882. She wrote of that occasion:

> I was at 6 o'clock Mass at St. Jacques, in the chapel of Our Lady of Mount Carmel, with Papa and Marie. Suddenly there was a very clear light in my soul and God showed me plainly that he did not want me at the Visitation but in Carmel... I had never thought of Carmel and now I suddenly found myself drawn irresistibly.

The statue before which Pauline received this revelation can now be seen in the Cathedral of St. Pierre.

THE PUBLIC GARDENS
Le Jardin de l'Evêche

Thérèse crossed these gardens every day on her way to school and each time she visited her uncle's home.

The entrance to the public gardens can be found across a courtyard at the top of the market square. They are near to the **post office**, where Thérèse went every morning after Mass at the end of 1887, when she was hoping for a letter from the Bishop giving her permission to enter Carmel. The public Gardens were originally the gardens of the Bishop's Palace which is now the Palace of Justice.

It was when she was crossing these gardens one evening after visiting her uncle's home, that Thérèse said, to her father, *My name is written in Heaven.* She had noticed the stars forming the letter 'T'.

THE GUERIN PHARMACY

Home of Isidore and Céline Guérin from 1866-1889, and birthplace of their children.

The original building of the Guérin Pharmacy was destroyed in the 1944 raids, but a pharmacy still stands on the same site to this day and it has been reconstructed in a similar style. It can be found on the corner of the market square, where Place Thiers meets rue Henry Chéron (known in their day as Place St. Pierre and Grande Rue).

Thérèse spent her first night in Lisieux at the pharmacy and later often spent Sunday evenings there. She wrote:

> *Papa, to please Uncle, used to permit Marie or Pauline to spend Sunday evenings at his home; I was happy when I was there with one of them. I*

preferred this to being invited all alone because then they paid less attention to me. I listened with great pleasure to all Uncle had to say, but I didn't like it when he asked me questions. I was very frightened when he placed me on his knee and sang Blue Beard in a formidable tone of voice. I was happy to see Papa coming to fetch us.

THE GUERIN HOUSE
19 rue Paul Banaston.

Home of the Guérin family from 1889 and temporarily of Léonie, Céline and their father after the lease on Les Buissonnets expired.

At the end of 1888 Isidore Guérin sold his pharmacy and retired from business. He bought this house (then 19, rue de la Chaussée) and Léonie and Céline went to live there; the lease on Les Buissonnets expired at the end of 1889. At this time Louis Martin was in hospital at Caen, but when he returned to Lisieux in May 1892 he stayed here for a short time.

THE MARTIN HOUSE
7 rue Labbey.

Home of Louis, Léonie and Céline.

This house opposite the back gate of the Guérin house was rented by the Martin family in July 1892 after Louis returned from hospital. The close proximity of the two houses meant that Céline was able to push her father across to the Guérin garden in his wheel chair.

THE BASILICA

**The Basilica was built in order to accommo-
date the large crowds of pilgrims visiting
Lisieux. Work began on it in 1929. It was
built in the neo-gothic style and was finally
consecrated on July 11th. 1954.**

Going up the hill, from the centre of the town, the Basilica is
on the right of the avenue Sainte Thérèse. In Thérèse's time
this was a narrow little lane leading up to the cemetery and a
favourite place for family walks.

The Basilica of St. Thérèse dominates Lisieux, standing on
a hillside overlooking the town. It gives a striking greeting to
the pilgrim arriving by train from Paris and one of the best
general views of the Basilica can be seen from the railway
station. This is very appropriate as Thérèse herself first
arrived in Lisieux by train from Alençon. The bell tower
stands apart from the main building of the Basilica.

The upper church is normally approached up the steps at
the front, but there is also an entrance up a ramp to the north
side of the building, turn to the left past the car park (follow
the sign 'Chemin de Croix'), going towards the outside Way
of the Cross. The upper church seats 4,000 people all of whom
have a clear view of the high altar. Mosaics and stained glass
windows present the theme of God's merciful love for us and
our response to that love. People from all over the world
subscribed to build this magnificent Basilica in honour of
St. Thérèse. It is a fitting monument to one who lived a
hidden life and taught a little way, showing how God raises
the lowly and how He reveals that which is hidden for His
own good purpose. There are eighteen chapels around the
Basilica each donated in thanksgiving by a different country.
The Blessed Sacrament is reserved in the first chapel to the
left of the high altar.

On the south (right) side about half way down is the
reliquary, given by Pope Pius XI, containing the two bones

The Basilica.

*In the crypt of the Basilica, a mosaic depicting
Thérèse's First Holy Communion.*

The graves of Louis and Zélie Martin, behind the Basilica.

*The Cemetery.
The cross which marks the
place of Thérèse's
original grave.*

of St. Thérèse's right arm, the arm with which she wrote her three manuscripts, later comprising *The Story of a Soul,* which has brought graces to so many people. Pilgrims come here to pray and to light their votive candles. The candles can be bought at the main door of the Basilica and by the reliquary.

To the right of the reliquary is the secretariat, the office where it is possible to arrange to have Masses offered for your intentions. In France the Mass offering is fixed by the diocese and at present (1993) in the Bayeux-Lisieux diocese one Mass is 75F and a novena of Masses is 750F.

The Basilica was miraculously preserved during the 1939-1945 war, as were Carmel, Les Buissonnets and the Cathedral. Although the Basilica, not then completed, was for a time used by the occupying German forces; it was later used as a refuge by two of Thérèse's own sisters, Pauline and Céline, when with the entire Carmelite Community, they took shelter in the crypt for three months during the 1944 air raids.

The crypt entrance is immediately before the steps going up to the main entrance of the Basilica. The crypt is much smaller than the upper church and the walls are adorned with beautiful mosaics, five of them show scenes from Thérèse's life. The statue of St. Thérèse behind the main altar is one by Father Marie-Bernard and together with the mosaic behind it is especially striking. The pillars down the centre aisle depict the beatitudes. Silence should always be observed in the crypt, where pilgrims are encouraged to spend time in private prayer. The Blessed Sacrament is reserved in the chapel of the Child Jesus. On the other side of the main altar is the chapel of the Virgin of the Smile. It was here that the Carmelites lived for eighty days during the 1944 raids and this was the altar they used.

The twelve side altars are dedicated to saints for whom Thérèse had a special love.

It is sometimes possible to climb to the dome. From this great height you can see all over Lisieux and will be able to pick out

Lisieux – The Basilica

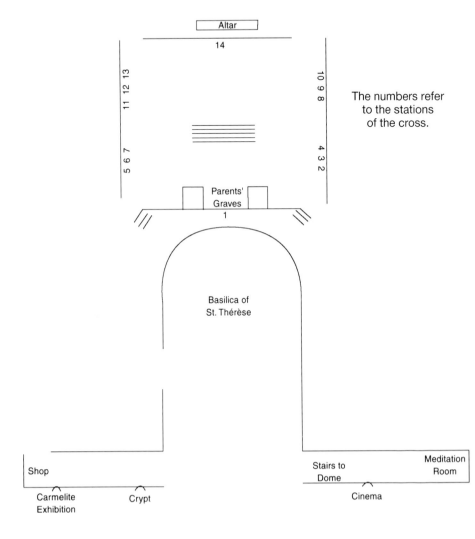

Altar

14

11 12 13

10 9 8

The numbers refer
to the stations
of the cross.

5 6 7

4 3 2

Parents'
Graves

1

Basilica of
St. Thérèse

Shop

Carmelite
Exhibition

Crypt

Stairs to
Dome

Cinema

Meditation
Room

Carmel, which is surrounded by trees; to the right of Carmel is the church of St. Jacques, and immediately behind the church you will see the Cathedral. Looking in the opposite direction you can see St. Thérèse's statue in the cemetery. Back to ground level behind the Basilica is the Way of the Cross. Beneath each station a quotation from St. Thérèse's writings is given in French, English and Spanish. The first station is found in front of the steps, the others are set out in groups of three, until the last station which is found beneath the large outdoor altar and crucifix. Also behind the Basilica are the graves of St. Thérèse's parents, Louis and Zélie Martin. Their remains were transferred here from the town cemetery in October 1958; their cause for beatification had been introduced the previous year. The cause took a major step forward on March 26th, 1994 when Pope John Paul II proclaimed the decree affirming their heroic virtues, enabling them to be called Venerable. The only requirement now for their beatification is for a proven miracle through their joint and sole intercession. Above their graves is a statue of St. Thérèse and words which she wrote in a letter to Abbé Bellière two months before she died; *God gave me a father and a mother more worthy of Heaven than of earth.*

An audio guide is available inside the Basilica, in eight languages and a small guide book by Mgr. Durand gives details of exterior sculptures, and the mosaics and windows inside the Basilica.

There is a meditation room at the far end of the south cloister. For this turn left as you leave the Basilica or turn right for the repository which is at the far end of the north cloister.

A missionary exhibition can be seen in the bell tower and a Carmelite exhibition can be seen under the north cloister, the entrance is near that of the crypt.

A film of St. Thérèse's life can sometimes be seen under the south cloister and on summer evenings there is usually a presentation in the main Basilica.

THE BELVEDERE
21, rue des Champs Remouleux.

This old timbered building, recognisable from a distance by its turret, houses various exhibitions on the life of the Church in the world of today. It reminds us that St. Thérèse is Patroness of all Missions and Missionaries and of her concern for the whole Church.

THE CEMETERY

Original burial place of St. Thérèse. It contains the graves of members of her family and others who knew her.

To reach the cemetery continue on up the Avenue Sainte Thérèse past the Basilica, joining the Avenue Jean XXIII. About one kilometre beyond the Basilica you will find the Cemetery on your right. The directions below are given from the first entrance past the Basilica. There is car parking further up the hill and another entrance to the cemetery.

In her testimony at Thérèse's tribunal for Beatification Céline said: *Sister Thérèse's body was buried publicly in Lisieux cemetery; hers was the first grave in the new plot acquired by the Carmel.*

Immediately after passing through the cemetery gate, at the bottom of the steps at the end of the slope, turn left, then keep straight along on the same level. A little way along, (approximately 100 metres), to your left you will see the grave of the Martin family. It is marked with a large round stone cross which is surrounded by yew trees. The monument carries the inscription *Famille Martin. O Crux Ave, Spes unica! La race des justes sera bénie.* (Hail Holy Cross, Our only hope! The race of the just will be blessed). After the death of Thérèse's father in 1894, Isidore Guérin had the family grave moved from Alençon and it was here that both

Thérèse's parents rested until their exhumation on October 13th. 1958. It is still the grave of Grandmother Martin, Grandfather Guérin and Thérèse's four little brothers and sisters who died in infancy.

Marie Hélène, born October 13th. 1864, died February 22nd. 1870
Marie Joseph Louis, born September 20th. 1866, died February 14th. 1867
Marie Joseph Jean Baptiste, born December 19th. 1867, died August 24th. 1868
Marie Melanie Thérèse, born August 17th. 1870, died October 8th. 1870

Thérèse tells how she turned to these little ones when she was still suffering from scruples after her eldest sister, Marie, entered Carmel:

No longer able to confide in Marie I turned towards Heaven. I addressed myself to the four angels who had preceded me there, for I thought that those innocent souls, having never known troubles nor fear, would have pity on their poor little sister who was suffering on earth. I spoke to them with the simplicity of a child, pointing out that being the youngest of the family, I was always the most loved, the most covered with my sisters' tender cares, that if they had remained on earth they, too, would have given me proofs of their affection. Their departure for Heaven did not appear to me as a reason for forgetting me; on the contrary, finding themselves in a position to draw from the divine treasures, they had to take peace for me from those treasures and thus show me that in Heaven they still knew how to love! The answer was not long in coming, for soon peace came to inundate my soul with its delightful waves, and I knew then that if I was loved on earth, I was also loved in Heaven. Since that moment,

The Cemetery:
The Martin family grave where the four little brothers
and sisters of Thérèse are buried.

my devotion for my little brothers and sisters has grown.

A little further along you will come to a flight of steps on your left, climb these steps and turn right, following the path along by the hedge. You will see a white statue of St. Thérèse and to the right, behind it, a wooden cross encased in glass. The cross marks the place of Thérèse's original grave. She was buried here on October 4th, 1897. Here the first pilgrims came to pray at her grave and the first miracles took place. The cross has been cleaned and restored, the words on it were written by Pauline, *I want to spend my Heaven doing good on earth.* Words Thérèse had said to her in July 1897. On September 6th, 1910 Thérèse's body was exhumed from this grave and placed in a cemented vault beneath the place where the white statue now stands. Thérèse's remains rested here until March 25th. 1923 when they were transferred to her Shrine in Carmel. Also buried in this plot are Thérèse's Prioress, Mother Marie de Gonzague, her novice mistress, Sister Marie of the Angels and some of the sisters instructed by Thérèse in the novitiate. Their names can be seen at the foot of the white statue. This plot is still in use and more recent Carmelite graves can also be seen.

It was Thérèse's uncle, Isidore Guérin, who bought the plot for Carmel next to his own. The name of his younger daughter, Sister Marie of the Eucharist, can be seen on the base of the white statue facing her family grave. The Guérin-Fournet-La Néele grave stands next to the white statue and contains the bodies of Thérèse's uncle, Isidore Guérin, (1841-1909), his wife Céline, née Fournet (1847-1900) and his daughter and son-in-law, Jeanne (1868-1938) and Francis La Néele (1858-1916).

Going back down the flight of steps you will find yourself in the area of the cemetery where many priests are buried. Turn along the first path to your left, the fourth grave along is the grave of Abbé Alcide Ducellier, (1849-1916), a priest at the Cathedral of St. Pierre. He heard Thérèse's first confession and remained her confessor until she began school at the

Benedictine Convent. He was one of those who gave his testimony at the tribunal for Thérèse's beatification. Thérèse writing about her first confession said:

> I made my confession in a great spirit of faith, even asking you (Pauline) if I had to tell Father Ducellier I loved him with all my heart as it was to God in person I was speaking... Father encouraged me to be devout to the Blessed Virgin and I promised myself to redouble my tenderness for her.

The grave of Canon Delatröette (1818-1895), parish priest of St. Jacques and Ecclesiastical Superior of the Lisieux Carmel, is along the path continuing straight on from the steps; it is the third grave on the left past the place where the paths cross. It was Canon Delatröette who opposed Thérèse's entry to Carmel at such an early age, but he was finally won over to appreciate her during the influenza epidemic of 1892, when for a time he allowed her to receive Holy Communion daily, an unusual privilege at that time. He was at last able to say of Thérèse, *She shows great promise for this Community.*

St Denis-Sur-Sarthon
Statue of St. Thérèse which marks her mother's birthplace.

St. Ouen-le-Pin. Mme. Fournet's home where Thérèse stayed in 1883, 1884 and 1885.

St. Ouen-le-Pin. The farm-house which Thérèse sketched in 1884.

PLACES NEAR LISIEUX

SAINT-OUEN LE PIN

The village of Saint-Ouen le Pin is about 9 kms. from Lisieux. Take the N13 (west, past the Benedictine Convent) to the village of La Boissière, turn right along the D59, then left at the cross-roads to the village, the church is on the right.

Madame Fournet, Céline Guérin's mother, lived on a farm near this village. Thérèse stayed here during the summers of 1883 and 1884 and at the end of July 1885 when she was recovering from whooping cough. The Martin family often spent days here during September to gather hazelnuts and they usually came with the Guérins in a large wagon. On August 8th, 1884 Thérèse sketched the main building of the farm. It has changed very little since she was here; it is set in the beautiful Auge countryside. Céline said that they always enjoyed themselves very much here. She wrote: *At Saint-Ouen everything was rustic, even the dishes, and that*

St. Ouen-le-Pin

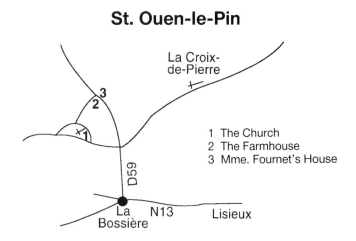

1 The Church
2 The Farmhouse
3 Mme. Fournet's House

pleased us... Thérèse was very much interested in the ponds and the little brook on the farm, and beyond the meadows a tiny little woods, perhaps a section of a former park called Le Theil. This woods was often the goal of our walks. We also went, but not very frequently, into the village by way of a pretty little road which was well shaded... The surrounding countryside was studded with castles which we could see in the distance.

Thérèse went to Mass in the village church when she was staying with Mme. Fournet. There is a statue of her in the churchyard.

Follow the lane to the left of the church, and this eventually leads you to the farmhouse which Thérèse sketched. It is just before the lane joins the main road (Roque-Baignard D59) on the right of the lane. Thérèse often walked this way to the church. The Fournet house where Thérèse stayed, now marked No. 5 Dunroain, is the first house round to the right on the main road.

THE CALVARY OF SAINT PIERRE

Returning from Saint-Ouen le Pin along the D59 towards La Boissière take a left turn at the cross roads along the D151 (towards Le Pré-d'Auge and Manerbe). Along this road, on your left, you will see a large crucifix, in a place known as La Croix-de-Pierre. The Martin family liked to walk here.

OUILLY LE VICOMTE

From Lisieux, continue past Les Buissonnets on the D579. On your right you pass the **Woods of Rocques** (Bois de Rocques). Thérèse often walked here with her family. About 3.5 Kms. from Lisieux you enter the village of Ouilly le Vicomte. Immediately after you pass the village sign and

Trouville. 'Pluie de Rose' the house at 29, rue de la Cavée where Thérèse stayed in 1886 and 1887.

The church at Ouilly-le-Vicomte which Thérèse sketched in 1887.

The church at Rocques which Thérèse used to visit with her father.

cross the bridge over the river La Pâquine, turn left along the D159 to the church. Thérèse sketched this church on April 12th, 1887, a year before she entered Carmel. A little further along this road there is a stream where Louis used to fish. This village was a favourite place for family walks and Thérèse liked to gather flowers in the fields.

ROCQUES

To reach this village take the D579 past the turn to Les Buissonnets. Then take the next right turn. About 3 Kms. on, you come to a cross roads, the Church is on your right. The stream, La Pâquine, where Louis used to fish is further along the same road. Thérèse used to walk here with her father and visit this beautiful old church. Unlike many of the country churches it is usually open. St. Thérèse's statue is inside to the right.

SAINT MARTIN DE LA LIEUE

This village is on the D579 about 4 Kms. from Lisieux towards Sées and Alençon. Just before you reach the village you pass the sixteenth-century Manor of Saint Hippolytus, it is on your right across a field. The River Touques runs in front of it and here Louis used to fish and Thérèse liked to gather flowers in the fields nearby. It was here on September 8th, 1879 that Louis caught a carp weighing 2.170 kgs. To find the church fork left in the village. On the main road just past the village looking back towards Lisieux you can see the Basilica in the distance.

BEAUVILLIERS

This village is on the D164 about 2 kms from Lisieux. The Martin family used to walk here and Louis would fish in L'Orbiquet. There is a beautiful view of the Basilica from the churchyard.

The Manor of Saint Hippolytus near St. Martin-de-la- Lieue. Louis used to fish in the river Touques which runs in front of the buildings.

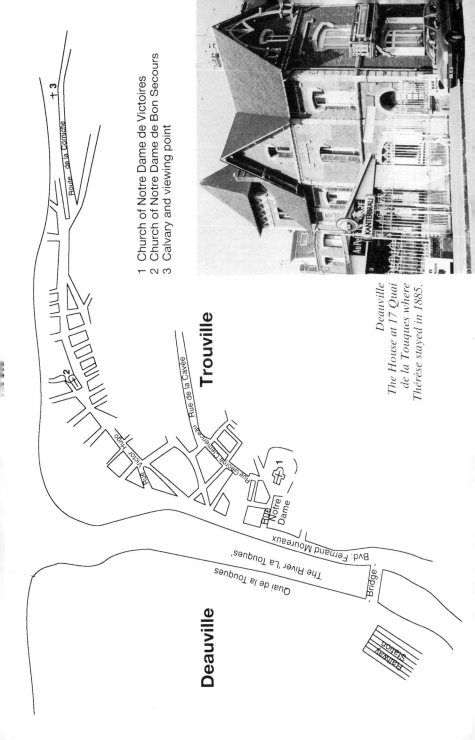

1 Church of Notre Dame de Victoires
2 Church of Notre Dame de Bon Secours
3 Calvary and viewing point

Deauville
The House at 17 Quai
de la Touques where
Thérèse stayed in 1885.

Trouville

Deauville

Route de la Corniche

Rue de la Cavée

Rue George Charpentier

Rue Victor Hugo

Rue Notre Dame

Bvd. Fernand Moureaux

The River 'La Touques'

Quai de la Touques

Bridge

Railway Station

TROUVILLE and DEAUVILLE

To reach Trouville and Deauville from Lisieux, take the D579 (north) to Pont l'Evêque. Passing near Pont l'Evêque we recall that this was another area where Louis came to fish in the Touques. On June 16th, 1887 Abbé Lepelletier, priest at Lisieux Cathedral and confessor to Louis and for a time to Thérèse, joined the fishing party, which consisted of Louis, Léonie, Céline and Thérèse. On that occasion he made a sketch of the three girls, showing Thérèse gathering flowers in a field. From Pont l'Evêque take the N177 to Trouville and Deauville.

There are regular train services between Lisieux and Trouville-Deauville. The journey is about 28 kms. One station serves the two towns which are divided only by the estuary of the Touques.

On August 8th, 1878 Thérèse visited the seaside for the first time. The Guérins had rented a villa, then known as Maison Leroux, in the Grande Rue, now known as **rue Georges Clémenceau**, at Trouville.

At a Calvary on Route de la Corniche, there is a **viewing point** across the sea and in the information given here it mentions that St. Thérèse first saw the sea at Trouville. She wrote of her visit:

> *I will never forget the impression the sea made on me; I couldn't take my eyes off it since its majesty,*

Trouville showing the church of Notre Dame de Victoires.

Window of St. Thérèse in
the church at Semallé.

Rose Taille's cottage at
Semallé where Thérèse lived
for 13 months with her
wet nurse.

the roaring of its waves, everything spoke to my soul
of God's grandeur and power.

In 1885 from May 3rd to 10th. Thérèse stayed with the Guérins at Deauville. The house where she stayed was known as Chalet des Roses and it can still be seen at **17, Quai de la Touques**, a plaque over the door recalls Thérèse's visit here. During her stay Thérèse made a sketch of the house. The café beside it stands where the Jardin Colombe was in Thérèse's time and it was here that she used to sit to sketch.

Later that same year, in September, Thérèse and Céline stayed with the Guérins at Villa Marie-Rose, 25, Rue Charlemagne, Trouville. This is now **25, rue Victor-Hugo**. Thérèse wrote of this visit:

Aunt provided us with all the amusement possible: donkey rides, fishing for eels, etc. I was still very much a child in spite of my twelve and a half years, and I remember the joy I had in putting on some pretty sky-blue ribbons Aunt had given me for my hair; I also recall having confessed at Trouville even this childish pleasure which seemed to be a sin to me.

This was at the time when Thérèse was suffering from scruples.

The church where she went to confession was **Notre Dame des Victoires**, which can be found at the top of rue Notre Dame. Thérèse often went here with the Guérin family. They also went to **Notre Dame de Bon Secours**, at the top of rue Victor Hugo. Both churches have statues of St. Thérèse.

In July 1886 Thérèse stayed again at Trouville with the Guérins, this time at Chalet des Lilas, **29, rue de la Cavée**. This house, now known as **Pluie de Rose**, is well marked, and is the best known of the houses Thérèse stayed in at the seaside. Thérèse returned here the next year, from June 20th to 26th 1887.

NOTRE-DAME DE GRACE

(Church of Our Lady of Grace, near Honfleur)

In remote countryside about 5 kms from Honfleur, on the estuary of the Seine, is the Church of **Notre-Dame de Grâce**. To reach the church follow the D513 from Deauville towards Honfleur, then turn left on to the D279 and left again on to the D62 following the signs to Côte de Grâce. After a left bend in the road you come to a wood and the Church of Notre-Dame de Grâce can be found down a short turning to your right.

Thérèse came here with her father, Léonie and Céline in July 1887 to beg Our Lady to obtain permission for her to enter Carmel.

On January 13th 1837, two young girls, the Gosselin sisters, came to this church with Father Sauvage to beg Our Lady to bless their project of founding a Carmel in Lisieux. The following year the Carmel of Poitiers made the foundation in Lisieux and accepted the two Gosselin sisters as postulants.

A short distance from the Church there is a large Calvary and a viewing point; from here it is possible to look across the estuary of the river Seine to Le Havre.

Both the Church of Our Lady of Grace and Le Havre were well known to the Martin family. On the occasion of their visit to Our Lady of Grace in July 1887 they went on to the International Exhibition at Le Havre. While they were there Thérèse bought Céline two little finches, but they both died the same month.

After Thérèse entered Carmel, her father who was already ill, left home one day, without telling anyone where he was going. Céline received a letter from him from Le Havre and on June 27th. she found him there and brought him back to Lisieux. Isidore Guérin and his nephew, Ernest Maudelonde, had accompanied Céline to Le Havre.

That same year on November 3rd Louis, Léonie and Céline went to Le Havre to meet Father Pichon who was leaving from the port there to return to Canada. On October 31st on their way to Le Havre they visited the Shrine of Our Lady of Grace at Honfleur.

Léonie's tomb in the crypt of the Visitation Convent at Caen.

he Church of Our Lady of race near Honfleur.

The Visitation Convent at Caen where Léonie spent her religious life from 1899-1941.

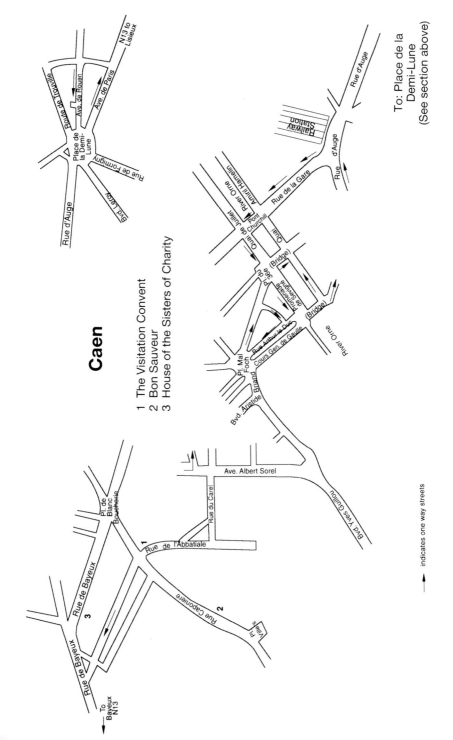

Caen

1 The Visitation Convent
2 Bon Sauveur
3 House of the Sisters of Charity

To: Place de la Demi-Lune
(See section above)

↑ indicates one way streets

CAEN

Caen is about 44 Kms. from Lisieux and is a straight journey along the N13 (west). It can also be reached by train from Lisieux.

THE VISITATION CONVENT
rue de l'Abbatiale

It was here that Léonie spent her religious life as Sister Françoise-Thérèse. Her tomb is in the crypt.

The Chapel is usually open and contains some beautiful stained glass windows depicting incidents from the lives of the Visitation Saints, St. Francis de Sales, St. Jane de Chantal and St. Margaret Mary. The Blessed Sacrament is reserved in a Chapel to the right of the High Altar, and St. Thérèse's statue stands in front of this Chapel. You will need to ask the sisters to let you into the crypt; ring the bell at the door in the courtyard, to the right of the Chapel entrance. The entrance to the crypt is outside, down steps on the left side of the Chapel and you will have to wait there for a sister to let you in. On the right as you enter the crypt you will see a glass case where many photographs and various objects connected with Léonie are displayed. There are two tombs in the crypt, Léonie's is in front of the tomb of the foundress of the monastery.

Léonie entered this convent first on July 16th 1887, but the following January she had to return home due to poor health. Thérèse visited her here in October 1887. Léonie entered again on June 24th 1893 but she had to leave again in 1895. She finally entered on January 28th 1899 when she was thirty six years old. She took the name Sister Françoise-Thérèse and lived the rest of her life here. She died on June 16th 1941.

Thérèse had predicted Léonie's vocation when she said to a Benedictine nun in Lisieux:

> *You must not worry about Léonie's failures to become a nun. When I am dead, she will enter the Visitation Order; she will persevere, and will take my name and that of St. Francis de Sales.*

BON SAUVEUR
rue Caponière

Louis was in hospital here from February 12th. 1889 until May 10th. 1892.

Some of the buildings of the hospital were destroyed in the Normandy raids but much of it still remains as it was in Louis' time. It is possible to visit the modern chapel and crypt.
Thérèse wrote:

> *I didn't know that on February 12th a month after my reception of the habit, our dear father would drink the most bitter and most humiliating of all chalices... Yet Papa's three years of martyrdom appear to me as the most lovable, the most fruitful of my life.*

ORPHANAGE OF SAINT VINCENT DE PAUL
59-61, rue de Bayeux

A week after Louis went into hospital Léonie and Céline arranged to take rooms here to be near their father, they stayed until the following June so that they could visit him frequently.

The Sisters of Charity are still in this building which is close to the hospital.

e Basilica of
tre-Dame-de-la-Délivrande
avourite place of pilgrimage
h the Martin family.

*Bayeux Cathedral from the garden
of the Bishop's Palace*

*The Bishop's Palace at Bayeux now
a museum of religious art*

*Our Lady of Grace where
Thérèse prayed in July 1887
for permission to be granted
for her to enter Carmel.*

*Bayeux Cathedral.
The Lady Chapel where
Thérèse prayed for the
success of her visit to
Bishop Hugonin.*

DOUVRES-LA-DELIVRANDE

NOTRE-DAME DE LA DELIVRANDE
Basilica of Our Lady
About 60 kms. from Lisieux, 13 kms. from Caen
and 3 kms. from Luc-sur-Mer

To reach Douvres-la-Délivrande from Lisieux (avoiding Caen) take the N13 (west) to Moult then turn right on to the D37. After crossing over the bridge at the Orne estuary turn right on to the D514 and follow the coast road through Luc-sur-Mer. As you approach Langrune-sur-Mer turn left on to the D7 to Douvres-la-Délivrande. As you enter the town the Basilica is facing you.

This ancient Shrine to Our Lady was a favourite place of pilgrimage with the Martin family. Set in a beautiful twin-spired Basilica the Blac'. Virgin holding the Child Jesus is still venerated today. St ues of St. Thérèse and St. John Eudes, who both came here as pilgrims, stand one each side of the church facing Our Lady's Shrine.

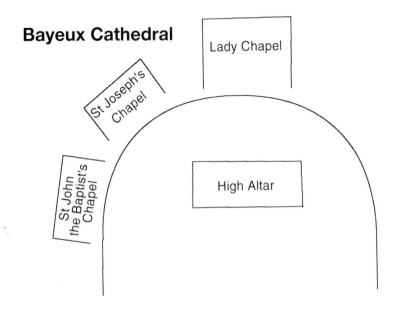

Bayeux Cathedral

Lady Chapel

St Joseph's Chapel

St John the Baptist's Chapel

High Altar

BAYEUX

About 70 kms. from Lisieux.
It is straight through on the N13
but follow the signs carefully around Caen.

Bayeux can be reached by train from Lisieux.

On October 31st. 1887, Thérèse went with her father to Bayeux to meet Bishop Hugonin. Thérèse was seeking his permission to enter Carmel at the age of fifteen.

THE CATHEDRAL
rue du Bienvenu

In the Chapel of St. John the Baptist, to the left of the High Altar, you will find St. Thérèse's statue and a photograph of her at the age of fifteen, with an account of her visit. In a glass case in the same Chapel there is a relic given by the Carmel of Lisieux. Another copy of the account of her visit, taken from *The Story of a Soul*, is displayed just outside the Lady Chapel. It was here that Thérèse prayed fervently for the success of her visit to the Bishop. When Thérèse and her father arrived in Bayeux, it was raining heavily so they took shelter in the Cathedral. An important funeral was taking place and Thérèse felt very embarrassed in her bright clothes, as her father took her past the mourners to a front seat. She was relieved when eventually she was able to pray quietly. Thérèse wrote:

Finally, I was able to breathe freely in a small chapel behind the main altar and stayed there a long time praying fervently and waiting for the rain to stop and allow us to leave. When we were leaving, Papa had me admire the beauty of the edifice which appeared much larger when empty, but one single thought occupied my mind.

The Blessed Sacrament is reserved in a chapel on the right side of the Cathedral.

THE BISHOP'S PALACE
rue Lambert-Leonard Le Forestier
Now a museum of religious art.

In one of the rooms of this museum you will notice many portraits of bishops on the walls. It is also still possible to look into the room where Thérèse had her meeting with Bishop Hugonin, the oval portrait of St. Thérèse hangs over the door of this room.

Thérèse wrote of her visit:

> *Father Révérony (the Vicar General) was very friendly... He had us traverse several huge rooms in which portraits of bishops were hanging on the walls... In the Bishop's study three enormous armchairs were set before the fireplace in which a bright fire was crackling away.*

Thérèse made her request to the Bishop but he did not give her a definite answer. In fact he eventually gave his permission by writing to the Prioress of Carmel at the end of the year.

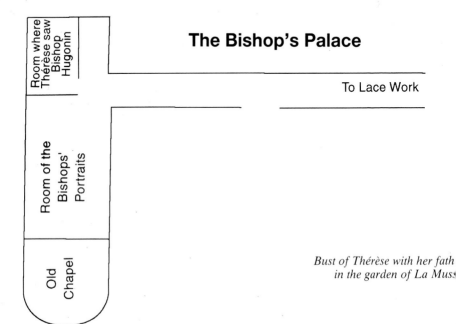

The Bishop's Palace

Room where Thérèse saw Bishop Hugonin

Room of the Bishops' Portraits

Old Chapel

To Lace Work

Bust of Thérèse with her fath in the garden of La Muss

A LA MÉMOIRE
DE
Monsieur Louis MARTIN
Père de Sainte THÉRÈSE
DE L'ENFANT-JÉSUS
DÉCÉDÉ LE 29 JUILLET 1894
AU CHÂTEAU DE LA MUSSE
ALORS PROPRIÉTÉ DE Mr GUÉRIN
SON BEAU-FRÈRE

LA MUSSE
(Near Evreux)

The Château La Musse, where Louis Martin died on July 29th 1894, is about 7 kms. from Evreux.

To reach La Musse from Lisieux take the N13 (east). Soon after you pass through the village of La Neuville turn right on to the D840 follow the by-pass around Conches-en-Ouche and take the D830 towards Evreux. La Musse is about 9 kms. on to your right, the drive runs off this main road. In recent years a hospital has been built in the grounds, and the buildings extend back from the road, nearly to the château. The name La Musse is displayed on a modern sign board.

The Lisieux-Paris train stops at Evreux and buses run from the town to La Musse.

It is still possible to walk through the woodlands and see the château where Louis died on July 29th. 1894. In the garden there is a bust of the young Thérèse with her father. Taking the path to the left of the château there is a superb view across the valley.

The Château of La Musse was jointly inherited by the Guérin and Maudelonde families. Louis, Léonie and Céline all spent time there on various occasions during the summer months. The château is surrounded by many acres of beautiful woodland and meadows. Louis was especially happy here. In a letter to her sister Jeanne, Marie Guérin wrote: *Uncle is radiant ever since he is here; he likes it better here than at Lisieux, he says. Céline and I have him take outings in the woods, but what pleases him very much is to look at the beautiful view. The other day he never grew tired of gazing at it, and he was laughing all day.*

ALENÇON

SAINT THERESE'S BIRTHPLACE
50, rue Saint-Blaise.

Thérèse was born here on January 2nd. 1873 and lived in this house until the family moved to Lisieux in November 1877, after the death of her mother.

This house held happy memories for Thérèse, she wrote:

God was pleased to surround me with love, and the first memories I have are stamped with smiles and the most tender caresses.

The sisters will guide you through the house but below are the main things you will see.

On entering the house you are in the hall. The stairs straight ahead of you are those which Thérèse's mother referred to in a letter to Pauline. She wrote: *Thérèse will not climb the stairs alone, but cries at each step, 'Mamma, Mamma!' If I forget to say, 'Yes, my child,' she stops and won't go any further.* Thérèse was probably thinking of these stairs when she told her novices to keep persevering, like a little child climbing a steep staircase.

Thérèse's mother, Zélie, was a lace maker, and in the room to your left you will see Zélie's worktable by the window. It was here that she received her lace workers and gave them the cotton to work their lace during the following week. She weighed the cotton on the scales you will see on the desk. In a bookcase on the wall there are leather-bound books won as prizes by Marie and Pauline when they were at school in the Visitation Convent in Le Mans. Beside the door is Louis' desk. Above the door is the crucifix given to the La Néeles as a wedding present from Louis and his daughters, and on the mantel-shelf is a clock set given to Céline and Isidore Guérin

St. Thérèse's birthplace in Alençon.

The staircase and original tiling in the birthplace of St. Thérèse at Alençon.

Zélie's work-table in the birthplace of St. Thérèse at Alençon.

A clock bought from Louis' shop and later given to the birthplace of St. Thérèse at Alençon.

Château La Musse where Louis Martin died on July 29th 1894.

Alençon

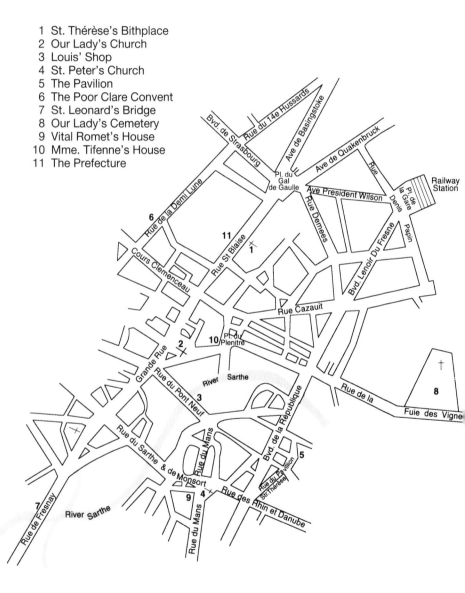

by the Martins for their wedding present. The small statue of Our Lady of Pontmain was probably brought back by Louis when he went there on pilgrimage. The small statue of St. Joseph is the one in front of which Zélie prayed for Thérèse, when as a baby, they feared for her life. As Rose fed her for the first time Thérèse recovered. (See page 88). There are a number of family photographs on display in this room.

In the adjoining room there is a case of family belongings, including some of Thérèse's toys, her grandfathers' medals, Louis' fishing bag, his spectacles and binoculars. On the mantel-shelf there is a beautiful clock which was bought from Louis' shop; later on the owner gave it as a souvenir to the house where St. Thérèse was born. On the walls there are some paintings done by Céline. This was the dining room. Behind it was the kitchen, in which exhibitions can be seen.

From the house you can visit the missionary exhibition in the crypt of the adjoining chapel.

Going through to the garden of the house you will see more exhibitions and Louis' fishing rods. Facing you is a statue of St. Thérèse. Behind it is a seat similar to the one on which Céline and Thérèse used to discuss their 'practices'. These were their sacrifices and acts of love which they talked about with such enthusiasm that a woman in the grocery store, prompted by a neighbour who had overheard these conversations, asked the maid, *What does Thérèse mean by these little practices? When she is playing in the garden that's all she talks about. Mme. Gaucherin listens at the window trying to understand what this debate about practices means!.* To the left you will see the tombstone which was placed on Zélie's first grave.

The chapel, which you enter from the steps outside, was built in 1925. Around it are painted six scenes from Thérèse's early life. On the right you can see into the room in which Thérèse was born and in which her mother died. The furniture is original.

Opposite is the Prefecture. Thérèse and Céline often used to go there to play with Genny Bechard, the Prefect's little daughter.

The room in which Thérèse was born and where her mother died.

Some of Thérèse's baby clothes displayed in the room where she was born.

Painting of Thérèse's baptism in the chapel adjoining St. Thérèse's birthplace.

LE BAPTEME DE Ste THÉRÈSE
DE L'ENFANT-JÉSUS

OUR LADY'S CHURCH
Church of Notre-Dame, Grande Rue.

Thérèse was baptised here on January 4th 1873, when she was two days old. Her parents were married here on July 13th. 1858 and it was in this church that Louis Martin offered himself as a victim in May 1888.

On the left as you enter is the Baptistry containing the font at which Thérèse was baptised. In a case is part of her baptismal robe. There is also a relic of the Saint here. The stained glass window above depicts her baptism, and other events in her life.

THE WATCHMAKER & JEWELLER'S SHOP
35, rue de Pont Neuf.

Here Louis established his business, he was a master watchmaker and jeweller. The Martin family lived here until July 1871.

Crossing the bridge, on your left, you will see No. 35. It is unmarked, but it was here that Louis had his watchmaker and jeweller's shop, the trade continues unchanged. The Martin family lived behind the shop and Louis' parents lived above. Here the first eight children were born.

SAINT PETER'S CHURCH
Place Saint-Pierre.

Louis and Zélie went to this church for the first thirteen years of their marriage and their children, with the exception of Thérèse, were all baptised here.

St. Pierre de Montsort is usually closed.

THE PAVILION
rue du Pavilion Ste. Thérèse.

Louis bought the Pavilion in 1857, he liked to spend time here alone. It was his retreat, in which he also kept his fishing tackle.

It is no longer possible to visit the inside of the pavilion, which is now privately owned, but it can still be seen from the outside. There is a statue of St. Thérèse above the gate.

THE POOR CLARE CONVENT
rue de la Demi-Lune.

It was here that Zélie, a Franciscan tertiary, used to go to her meetings. Here too Léonie tried her vocation, but her health was not good enough to live the life of the Poor Clares.

The chapel of this convent is usually open.

The Pavilion, Alençon.

Our Lady's Cemetery, Alençon

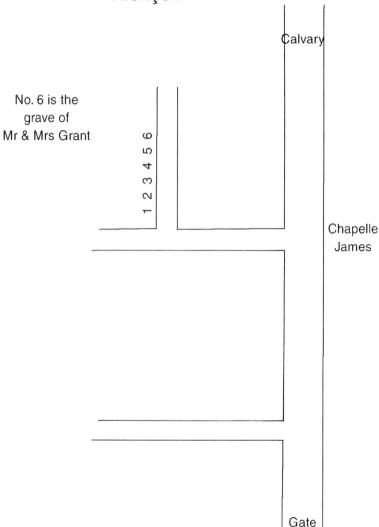

Calvary

No. 6 is the
grave of
Mr & Mrs Grant

1 2 3 4 5 6

Chapelle
James

Gate

Louis' watchmaker and jewellers' shop at Alençon.

SAINT LEONARD'S BRIDGE

rue de Fresnay

**It was here that St. Thérèse's parents first
met.**

Passing St. Leonard's Church and the entrance to the hospital
you will find yourself on a bridge over the river.

It was here that Zélie noticed Louis passing by and heard
an interior voice which said: *This is he whom I have prepared
for you.*

OUR LADY'S CEMETERY

Cimetière Notre-Dame,
rue de la Fuie des Vignes.

**Here Zélie was first buried and so were the
four children who died in infancy, but Isidore
Guèrin had their grave moved to Lisieux in
1894 when Louis died.**

It was to this cemetery that Thérèse came when she visited
Alençon in August 1883. She wrote of her visit:

> *My joy was very great when seeing the places where
> I had spent my childhood days and especially when
> I was able to pray at Mamma's grave and ask her to
> protect me always.*

The grave of Mr. and Mrs Grant, for many years custodians
of St. Thérèse's birthplace, can be seen here. Mr. Grant was
a Scottish Presbyterian minister, converted to Catholicism by
St. Thérèse.

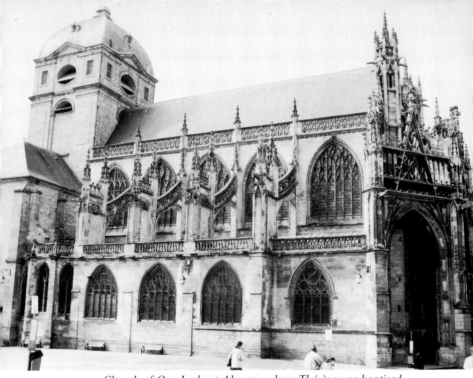

Church of Our Lady at Alençon where Thérèse was baptised and her parents married.

St. Leonard's Bridge, Alençon, where Thérèse's parents first met.

VITAL ROMET'S HOUSE
72, rue du Mans

This large house, still privately owned, was very well known
to the Martin family. Vital Romet was a pharmacist in
Alençon and his sister Pauline lived with him. Vital was
Céline's Godfather and Pauline was Pauline's Godmother.
The relationship between the families was so close that the
Martin girls called Pauline Romet 'Aunt Pauline' although
they were not related. The Catholic Circle, of which Louis
was a member, met in this house. After the Martin family
moved to Lisieux they sometimes stayed with the Romets at
this house when visiting Alençon.

MADAME TIFENNE'S HOUSE
6, Place du Plénitre

This house is also privately owned and like the Romet house
was very well known to the Martin family. After they moved
to Lisieux it was here that they stayed on their visits to
Alençon when they did not stay with the Romets. On one
occasion Thérèse shared a room here with Céline and she
referred to this bedroom as the 'Cardinal's room' because
it was decorated with red wallpaper and hangings. Léonie
Gilbert, who on marriage became Madame Tifenne, was
Léonie's Godmother. Her husband was a pharmacist who
had done some of his training with Isidore Guérin. The
Gilbert family lived on rue du Pont Neuf opposite Louis'
shop, so they were all known well to the Martin family. In
September 1888 Madame Tifenne, with her husband, her
niece, Thérèse Gilbert, and her nephew, Pierre, visited
Thérèse in the parlour at Carmel. After Thérèse's death,
when Madame Tifenne had read *The Story of a Soul*, she
wrote to Thérèse's sisters in Carmel, *It was with heartfelt
interest that I read all the details given about your family
and ancestors. Those whom I knew, together with your father*

and your saintly mother, made me realise what a line of saints you possess in your family. Madame Tifenne was over eighty when she died in 1929. She is buried in Our Lady's Cemetery.

When the Martin family stayed at Alençon in August 1883 Madame Tifenne took them to visit her sister Madame Monnier at **Grogny** which is about 10 kms. from Alençon, south along the N138 to Arçonnay, and turning right along Chemin de Haute Eclair. Grogny is behind le Château de la Chevalerie along a little road to the right. It was here that Thérèse rode side-saddle. Of this visit Thérèse wrote: *I must admit this life had its charms for me.*

Pierre Romet's Château at St. Denis-sur-Sarthon.

Trouville:
The confessional in Notre Dame de Victoires where
Thérèse went in 1885 to confess her scruples
over the blue hair ribbon.

SEMALLE

Thérèse spent thirteen months here living in a small farm cottage with her wet nurse Rose Taillé, her husband Moses and their four children.

The village of Semallé is about 9 kms. from Alençon. Take the N12 out of Alençon towards Paris, turn left on to the D307 this will bring you to the church. To reach the cottage continue on the D307 until you reach a T junction; there is a cemetery opposite, turn right, and it is signposted from here. You will quickly take a left turn, then a right turn to the cottage.

Buses run from Alençon along the main road past the turn to Semallé.

In **the parish church** there is a window of St. Thérèse. She is portrayed holding the veil of the Holy Face. Behind her is Rose Taillé's cottage and Redskin, the cow on which Rose used to tie Thérèse to free her arms for milking.

Rose Taillé's cottage, about 2 kms. from the village can be seen from outside, and a plaque and small statue of St. Thérèse recall her stay here, from March 1873 until April 1874.

Continuing along the N12 from Alençon towards Paris just past the left turn (D307) to Semallé you pass the entrance to **Lanchal Manor**, Thérèse visited the Rabinal family here when she was ten years old.

Plaque and statue on Rose Taillé's cottage at Semallé.

88

SAINT DENIS SUR SARTHON

**St. Thérèse's mother, Zélie Guérin, was born
here and baptised in the village church.**

The village of Saint Denis sur Sarthon is about 8 kms from
Alençon. It is on the N12. Take this road from Alençon
towards Pré-en-Pail.

Buses run from Alençon along the main road and through
the village of St. Denis sur Sarthon.

Turn left in the village to reach the church, which is usually
open. There is a statue of St. Thérèse in the baptistry and
you can see the font at which Zélie was baptised. A little
further along the main road (N12) on your left you will see
another statue of St. Thérèse, this marks the place of her
mother's birth.

As you approach the village of Saint Denis sur Sarthon,
along the road from Alençon, look to your left after you
pass the village sign, but before you reach the centre of the
village. You will see **Pierre Romet's Château**. This château
is privately owned but can be easily seen from the entrance

St. Denis-sur-Sarthon
The church where Zélie was baptised.

Semallé & St. Denis-Sur-Sarthon

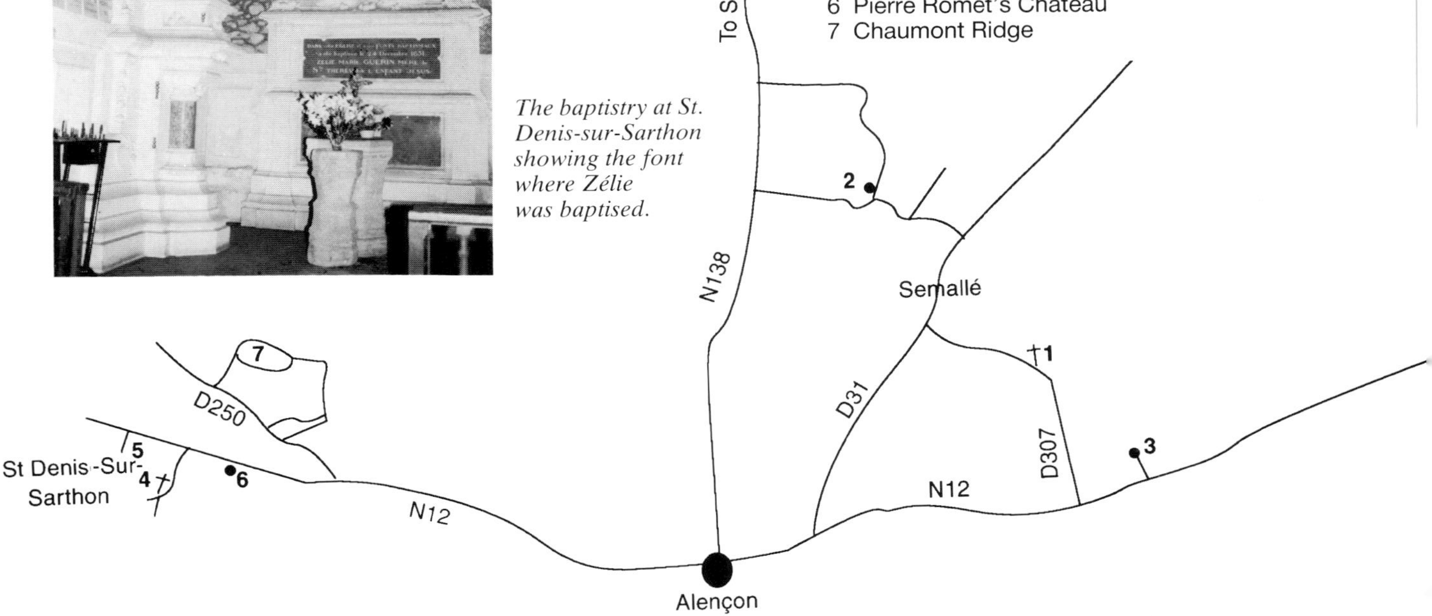

1 Semallé Church
2 Rose Taille's Cottage
3 Lanchal
4 St. Denis-Sur-Sarthon Church
5 Birthplace of Zélie Guérin
6 Pierre Romet's Château
7 Chaumont Ridge

The baptistry at St. Denis-sur-Sarthon showing the font where Zélie was baptised.

To Sées

N138

Semallé

N12

D31

D307

3

2

Alençon

N12

D250

7

6

5 St Denis-Sur-Sarthon

4

The Church at St. Denis-sur-Sarthon.

gates. Pierre was the brother of Vital and Pauline Romet. Thérèse visited this château when she was ten years old. The family were staying in Alençon. Thérèse wrote of that visit:

> *I can say it was during my stay at Alençon that I made my first entrance into the world. Everything was joy and happiness around me; I was entertained, coddled, and admired; in a word, my life during those two weeks was strewn only with flowers... At the age of ten the heart allows itself to be easily dazzled, and I consider it a great grace not to have remained at Alençon.*

Near Saint Denis sur Sarthon is the **Chaumont Ridge**. It can only be reached by a steep climb. There is a Calvary and a viewing point but in Louis' time it was the home of a well known 'thaumaturgus', (a miracle worker) who it was claimed cured all sorts of fever patients. Louis went there to pray for Marie's cure when she was suffering from typhoid fever.

ROULEE

About 9 kms from Alençon, near La Fresnaye, on the D16 is the village of Roulée.

After Louis sold his watchmaker and jewellers shop he invested some of his money in the area around Alençon and he bought some land in this village. The story is told in Marie's obituary of how she was walking with her father here at the end of the summer holidays.

> *Marie began to gather some flowers saying, 'I will take these back to the Visitation School as a souvenir of Roulée'. Her father, wishing to teach her a lesson, replied, 'That's it! And then you can look down on your little friends by showing them the flowers from your estate'. Poor Marie, seeing that he had guessed her thoughts, threw away her bouquet to show that she was above vainglory.*

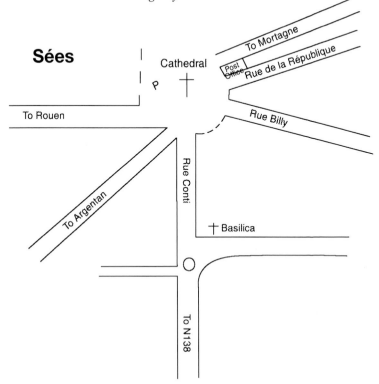

SEES

Alençon is in the diocese of Sées, or Séez, as it was previously spelt. The twin spires of the Cathedral can be seen from the train travelling between Lisieux and Alençon.

Trains stop at Sées and it is a short journey from Alençon, (about 22 kms) but the railway station is on the outskirts of the town. By road take the N138 from Alençon to Sées.

THE CATHEDRAL

This beautiful thirteenth-century Cathedral stands in the centre of the town. Thérèse came here on pilgrimage and there is a modern wooden statue of her in the Chapel of St. Godegrand, on the left of the Blessed Sacrament Chapel, behind the High Altar.

Sées Cathedral

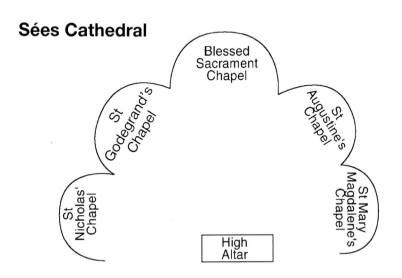

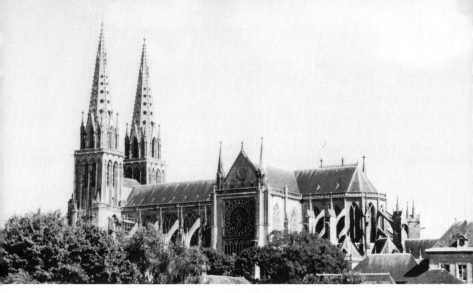

Sées Cathedral.

THE BASILICA
OF THE IMMACULATE CONCEPTION

Louis often came here on pilgrimage. It was the first church to be dedicated under this title, shortly after the proclamation of the doctrine of the Immaculate Conception (1854) and Our Lady's appearances to Bernadette at Lourdes (1858). Zélie, brought Léonie here as part of her preparation for her First Holy Communion.

ABBAYE DE LA TRAPPE

Louis came here on retreat.

It is about 36 kms from Sées. To reach the Abbey take the D3 from Sées to Moulins-la-Marche, then the D32 to Soligny-la-Trappe, turn left along the D251, from here the Abbaye La Trappe is well signposted.

This Abbey is near the town of Soligny-la-Trappe and it is

Abbaye de la Trappe.

sometimes referred to as La Trappe of Mortagne, though in fact it is some distance from that town.

Céline wrote, *Our father used to make closed retreats. At the Trappist Monastery of Soligny they have on record the dates of one of his stays there.*

Father Marie-Bernard, (Louis Richomme, 1883-1975) entered this monastery. He had a great devotion to St. Thérèse and made many beautiful statues of her. His work includes the recumbent statue in her Shrine at Carmel in Lisieux, the statue outside Carmel, the statue above the altar in the Basilica Crypt at Lisieux and the one outside the Basilica. The statue in the bapistry of Our Lady's Church in Alençon is also his work and many others, including the one in the Church at La Trappe.

It is usually possible to visit the church which is to the right at the front of the monastery. It is sometimes possible to see a film on the life and work of the monks. To the right of the building there is a large car park and on that side there is a gift shop selling pottery and other goods made by the monks. Many people visit La Trappe to collect St. Bernard's water. This is pure spring water which the monks have made available to everyone.

The Theresian Trust

Charity No. 288623

The Theresian Trust was founded in 1984 to promote the teaching and example of Saint Thérèse of Lisieux and the life and ideals of the Martin family.

The Theresian Trust was opened in Birmingham, England in 1987 and houses an extensive reference library and a lending library, together with exhibitions and display books.

There is also a small chapel where the Divine office is said each day and where prayer requests are placed in an envelope in front of Saint Thérèse's statue and remembered after the mid-day Angelus. In the garden there is a hermitage, just big enough for one person.

Books, cards and cassette tapes on the life and teaching of Saint Thérèse and her family are offered for sale.

Most important of these is *The Story of a Soul**, Saint Thérèse's own account of her life, originally published as her obituary, and now translated into over forty languages.

Also available are her *Letters* and *Last Conversations*; the CTS booklet *The Parents of Thérèse of Lisieux – were they saints?* by Christine Frost; and *St. Thérèse of Lisieux* by Christine Frost – (Anthony Clarke).

For a full sales list, lending library list and further information on the work of the Trust, contact The Theresian Centre, 617 Church Road, Yardley, Birmingham, B33 8HA, England. Telephone Birmingham 783 2850.

* Translated by John Clarke, published by ICS
  Translated by Michael Day, published by Anthony Clarke.